KEITH DORRICOTT

Going Deeper

Contents

Preface

The objective of this short course is that we will "launch out into the deep" - that is move to a level in our experience with God — just like Peter did in Luke chapter 5. Jesus said to Peter *"Launch out into the deep and let down your nets for a catch."* Despite having fished all night and caught nothing, Peter obeyed. They caught so many fish that the nets started to break and two boats were almost sunk. When Peter saw this he said, *"Depart from me, for I am a sinful man, O Lord."* Jesus replied *"Do not be afraid. From now on you will catch men."*

The course comprises 4 modules:

1. 'THE OFFENCE OF THE CROSS" - To realize the impact of the cross of Christ on us as disciples - what an irreversible change it made to us, and how we died with Christ to be freed from the power of sin within us - we will learn about ourselves (just as Peter did), our sinful nature, and the only remedy - we will learn how essential it is to make an irreversible decision to follow Him and not the world, and to make a public stand for Him.

2. "LIFE TO THE FULL" - To realize the fullness of the eternal life that we have been given and how to start enjoying it to the full right now - how this involves us (like Peter) deepening our knowledge of God and witnessing His power through us

in service - and how to make it a consistent reality in our day-to-day lives.

3. "PRESSING ON TOWARDS THE GOAL" - To understand what it will take to persevere to the end, to finish the race, to reach the goal, to win the prize, by surrendering (like Peter) in total obedience - how to overcome the setbacks that we all face, such as discouragement, suffering and temptation.

4. "SALT AND LIGHT" - To accept our mission for the Lord (as Peter did) to influence those around us, to reflect Christ in our world - how to be a deterrent to evil, how to be an influence for good, and how to shine the light on this world's ignorance of God.

The writer to the Hebrews urged them not to settle for mediocrity in their lives for Cod He said in Hebrews 6:1: "Therefore, leaving the discussion of the elementary principles of Christ let us go on to perfection..."

The height of a tree is determined by the depth of its root. It is the root that bears the fruit. Depth matters. When we go deeper into the things of God, we get nearer to God Himself - which is all part of His plan in "sanctifying" us. He wants to draw us closer and closer to Himself. As we all come closer to Him, we thereby come closer to each other, just like the spokes on a wheel that meet at the centre.

"For the Spirit searches all things, yes, the deep things of God." (1 Corinthians 2:10)

1

Module 1 - The Offence of the Cross

"If I still preach circumcision, why do I still suffer persecution? Then the offence of the cross has ceased." (Galatians 5:11)

Our salvation was based on the work of Christ on the cross - you know that. But Christ's death happened a long time ago. How relevant is it now to your life as a disciple? Christ is no longer on the cross. Don't you have to move on to other things in your Christian life? No - the Bible makes it clear that the cross of Christ continues to be a central part of your ongoing life as a disciple of the Lord Jesus. If you are going to make progress - if you are going to "go deeper" in your experience with God, you will have to encounter the on-going effect of the cross on your life.

The only reason the cross was necessary in the first place was the fact of sin, which was the great impediment to us having a relationship with God our maker. Since we don't stop sinning when we get saved, the cross continues to be relevant. It is the only thing that overcomes sin. The apostle Paul, who was an experienced Christian, and who so understood how fully the cross affected his daily life that he referred to it as being crucified himself, said: "I have been crucified with Christ; it is no longer I who live, but Christ lives in me" (Galatians 2:20). The cross of Christ, therefore, is the foundation basis of your discipleship. We will examine how this is the case in this module. And it all begins with understanding what your baptism is all about.

Do You Understand What Your Baptism Meant?

The Bible teaches that your water baptism should follow soon after your salvation: *"Then those who gladly received his word were baptized"* (Acts 2:41). Why is this? Your baptism is your public declaration of your identification with Jesus Christ in His death at Calvary. It is the first step in taking a stand publicly for who is your Lord. (The early disciples were not expected to wear a crucifix or a badge to signify it; they were expected to be baptized and become part of a church of God as their public witness.) Christ's crucifixion is offensive to some people in the world because it demands that they acknowledge who He is, and that it was their sin that required His death. It was barbaric and extreme - an offence to human pride. But sin requires extreme measures. That's why the people Paul was preaching to didn't want to hear it and they persecuted him. He called it: *"The offence of the cross"* (Galatians 5:11).

It can possibly also be offensive to us as Christians because it demands an end to living for ourselves. A person who is being crucified: (i) has no future in that life; (ii) is facing only one way, the opposite of those who are crucifying him; and (iii) is experiencing the pain of giving up the life they once enjoyed. To what extent is this true of you?

Checkpoint: Are you a baptized believer?

```
Are you a believer in the Lord Jesus Christ (see Acts
16:31)? Have you then been baptized in water into the
name of the Father and of the Son and of the Holy
Spirit (see Matthew 28:19.20)? If not, please think
seriously about these verses and how they apply to
you. If so, then think back to your baptism and try
to grasp fully what it meant.
```

Romans 5

Israel was told to build a mound of stones after they had crossed the river Jordan into Canaan, the land of their inheritance. They were to return there on future occasions, with their children, to re-live the meaning of when they were "baptized" in the Jordan (Joshua 4). Their life after crossing the Jordan would be very different from life in the wilderness, which is all they had known. They would: (i) eat different food; (ii) live in different homes; and (iii) have different neighbours with whom they would be in constant conflict. What do you think are the parallels today in your life after baptism?

Romans 6

This chapter is all about the meaning of your baptism and how it characterizes the rest of your life as a disciple. For example it says:

> *"Do you not know that as many of us as were baptised into Christ Jesus were baptized into His death? Therefore we were buried with Him through baptism into death, that just as Christ was raised from the dead by the glory of the Father even so we also should walk in newness of life. For if we have been united together in the likeness of His death, certainly we also shall be in the likeness of His resurrection, knowing this, that our old man was crucified with Him, that the body of sin might be done away with, that we should no longer be slaves of sin. For he who has died has been freed from sin"* (Romans 6:3-7).

What do the expressions *"baptized into His death"* and *"united ... in the likeness of His death"* mean? They are saying that your baptism was "like" His death, and that you were joined with Him in the effect of His death. It says, in effect, that your baptism was a funeral service, a burial. When you are buried, it proves that you're dead. But when and how did you die? For the answer to this, we'll need to look at two more expressions in these verses: *"our old man was crucified with Him"* and *"that the body of sin might be done away."* Your "old man" is your sinful nature that you have had from birth. It is rooted in your body, which makes it a "body of sin." At your salvation, you received a new, spiritual nature from God that can't sin (see 1 John 5:18). As a result, you now have two, totally different natures within you.

To prevent the old nature from being dominant, it had to be put to death. That requires an act of commitment and resolve on your part, to allow the death of Christ to apply to your old nature also, "the old you" - that the power of sin within you would not be allowed to be in control from then on. Your baptism was, in effect, you making a statement that, from that point on, the new spiritual life in you would be dominant in obedience to the Lord Jesus Christ.

What is "Dying with Christ"?

The first thing to realize is that "dying 'with' Christ" is not the same as Christ dying 'for' you. We're told in the previous chapter of Romans that: *"while we were still sinners, Christ died for us"* (Romans 5:8). The death of Christ paid the penalty for your sins, so that you would never have to be banished from the presence of God and suffer eternal punishment. But the death of Christ also dealt with what you are - you are a sinner and the power of sin is in your body, even after you receive eternal salvation.

Peter's relationship with the Lord was founded on the realization of what he was; he said *"Depart from me, for I am a sinful man, o Lord!"* (Luke 5:8). Similarly, your spiritual life requires that you constantly remember that you are inherently sinful and that you need your identification with the death of Christ to make possible the enjoyment of the life you have received.

The Divide of the Cross

For the Lord Jesus, there was no way around the cross of Calvary if He was to accomplish the purpose of God for which He had come. He knew fully in advance what it was going to cost Him. The night before His death He was in the garden of Gethsemane ... *"And being in agony He prayed more earnestly. Then His sweat became like great drops of blood falling down to the ground"* (Luke 22:44). He pleaded with His Father to see if there could be any other way but the cross: *"He went a little farther and fell on His face, and prayed, saying, "O My Father if it is possible, let this cup pass from Me"* ... but of course there wasn't. He completely surrendered His will to God's.

Checkpoint: The Cross as the Crossroads

```
"Nevertheless, not as I will but as You will"
(Matthew 26:39). Christ's experience in Gethsemane
exactly captures the essence of the meaning of the
cross of Christ in your life as a disciple, as well
as His: "... not as I will, but as You will." Have
you come to the crossroads of the cross in your own
life? Which way have you turned? Which path are you
on right now?
```

And so your first step as a disciple in following Christ as your Lord is to surrender your will totally to Him. A good example of this is the apostle Paul (Saul of Tarsus) who, as soon as he received Christ as his Saviour, said: *"Lord, what do you want me to do?"* (Acts 9:6). And so the cross is a "crossroads" - we have to choose which way to go, because we can't stay on both paths.

When Israel was at Sinai they went back to the Egyptian practice of idolatrous worship (Exodus 32). When Moses came down from the mountain from being with God, he ... *"saw that the people were unrestrained (for Aaron had not restrained them, to their shame among their enemies), then Moses stood in the entrance of the camp, and said, 'Whoever is on the Lord's side, come to me.' And all the sons of Levi gathered themselves together to him"* (Exodus 32:25-26). Each Israelite had to make a public decision - which side am I on? There was no middle ground. It is the same with you today. The cross demands that you choose one way or the other.

Checkpoint – Are You on the Fence?

Are you ever embarrassed about the cross and your identity as a follower of the person that the world crucified? Do you find it difficult to communicate to your friends your experience of salvation and discipleship in a relevant way?

Know – Reckon – Present

There are 3 things that Romans chapter 6 tells us to do, to put into practice every day the effect of our death with Christ to the power of sin in our lives. The key action words are: know, reckon, and present:

- **Know** (understand) - verse 6: *"knowing this, that our old man was crucified with Him, that the body of sin might be done away with, that we should no longer be slaves of sin."*
- **Reckon** (personalize it to yourself) - verse 11: *"reckon yourselves to be dead indeed to sin, but alive to God in Christ Jesus our Lord."*
- **Present** (act on it) - verse 13: *"do not present your members*

as instruments of unrighteousness to sin, but present yourselves to God as being alive from the dead, and your members as instruments of righteousness to God."

Know – do you understand that:

- You have an inherently sinful nature that doesn't disappear when you get saved and always wants to assert itself?
- Your baptism represented a declaration by you of your intention to end your old sinful life which was dominated by that self–seeking nature (which may not always seem bad to you), and live totally in the new life you've received?
- That the cross of Christ stands as a dividing line in your life?

Reckon - have you decided to personalize this reality by:

- Offering yourself unconditionally in a vow to the Lord (preferably in prayer)?
- Resolving to disconnect yourself from attractions and re-lationships that inhibit your whole-hearted obedience to the Lord and His Word, no matter how much they appeal to you"?
- Renewing this commitment periodically?

Present - are you putting this into practice day by day by:

- Consciously refusing to look at, listen to, say, sing, go to or do spiritually harmful things?
- Consciously choosing to look at, listen to, say, sing, go to or do scripturally obedient things?

Checkpoint - Deliverance from Sin

- What is the difference between a believer and a
disciple? (see Matthew 28:20)
- What are your own particular weaknesses and
tendencies to sin? (see Hebrews 12:1)
- How much do you want to be free from the influence
of things that please you but are displeasing to the
Lord? (see 1 John 2:1)
- Have you ever confessed to the Lord that the world
has been crucified to you and you to the world
(Galatians 6:14)?
- Is there an experience of being delivered from a
sinful habit that you can share with others for their
help?
How can you help others in your church experience
deliverance by the cross from their sinful tendencies?

How is Your Attitude?

One of the main ways that it will be evident that Romans chapter
6 is becoming a reality in your life is by a changed attitude to
things in the world around you (even legitimate things). The
apostle John wrote about this:

> "Do not love the world or the things in the world. If
> anyone loves the world, the love of the Father is not in
> him. For all that is in the world— the lust of the flesh,
> the lust of the eyes, and the pride of life— is not of the
> Father but is of the world. And the world is passing away,
> and the lust of it; but he who does the will of God abides

forever" (1 John 2:15-17).

Checkpoint — Survey Results

A recent survey of some young people concluded that
the biggest impediment to their churches being
stronger was "worldliness". In particular, different
standards of behaviour among young people in churches
was cited as a big stumbling-block.
- Do you agree with this? How can you and others help
to raise the standard of "godliness" in our churches
in face of this worldliness?
- Why is there such a big difference in practices
between our churches, in things like: tolerance of
drinking; social activities; suitable dress etc.?
This really weakens attempts to testify to other
believers about our unity of doctrine and practice.
- How big a problem in you maintaining a disciple
lifestyle is peer pressure?
- Are you willing to confront other people for their
wrong conduct and poor commitment? How can you do
this without it backfiring?

Loving the world includes many aspects of our lives. What examples can you think of where "the divide of the cross" makes a difference (or should make a difference) in your:

- Relationships
- Attitude to, and use of, money
- Entertainment
- Possessions
- Career

In Galatians 5:24, Paul said: *"those who are Christ's have crucified the flesh with its passions and desires."* Paul came to realize how incapable his flesh was, even at its best, in pleasing God. Why is it such a difficult thing for us to surrender control of our life to God, who is obviously so much more capable than we are? It is because of our "old man", our "flesh" (our old nature). We have to learn the difficult reality that no matter what we try, no matter how long we try, it is impossible to please God through our old nature; we have to learn that *"those who are in the flesh cannot please God"* (Romans 8:8). Trying to please God in the flesh is an impossibility. It will be a constant source of frustration.

In Galatians 6:14 Paul also said: *"God forbid that I should glory except in the cross of our Lord Jesus Christ, by whom the world has been crucified to me, and I to the world."* What do you think he meant by saying "the world has been crucified to me"? What do you think he meant by saying "and I to the world"?

Mind Renewal

Your life is shaped by what you think - what you understand, your attitudes, your values, your beliefs. The Bible expresses it this way: *"For as he thinks in his heart, so is he"* (Proverbs 23:7). Therefore any change in your behaviour first requires a change in your thinking. A changed attitude and a proper understanding of the things of God come about by having our minds "renewed." Our attitudes, our ideas, our beliefs and our values are shaped by the experiences we have had in our lives, arid what we have been exposed to - at home, in our education, at work, and elsewhere. A great deal of what we come to think is contrary to God's Word and so we need to have our mind renewed. Several scriptures refer to this:

- *"And do not be conformed to this world, but be transformed by the renewing of your mind"* (Romans 12:2);
- *"Be renewed in the spirit of your mind"* (Ephesians 4:23);
- *"Set your mind on things above, on the things of the Spirit"* (Colossians 3:2);
- *"with your mind serve the law of God"* (Romans 7:25);
- *"Let nothing be done through selfish ambition or conceit, but in lowliness of mind let each esteem others better than himself. Let this mind be in you which was also in Christ Jesus..."* (Philippians 2:3,5);
- *"... being like minded, having the same love, being of one accord, of one mind"* (Philippians 2:2);
- *"... bringing every thought into captivity to the obedience of Christ"* (2 Corinthians 10:5);
- *"... to be carnally minded is death, but to be spiritually minded is life and peace"* (Romans 8:6).

Checkpoint – Mind Renewal

Do these scriptures indicate that this is a passive or an active thing? What are the practical ways in which you can renew your mind? How long does it take?

What are some of the values and attitudes that are admired in the world, such as by celebrities and the media, that are totally contrary to the mind of the Lord? What in your opinion are the things on TV, the Internet, in the movies, in novels, and in popular music that are most polluting to a disciple's mind? We have been socialized since our birth and through school by the values and thinking of our world, which is why we need our minds renewed. What are some aspects of "conventional wisdom" in the world that are contrary to the mind of Christ ...

- In their language?
- In their sexuality?
- In their law-abiding?
- In their appearance?
- In their materialism?
- In their politics?
- In their attitude to money?
- In their attitude to voluntary bankruptcy?
- In their attitude to lotteries?
- In their attitude to feminism?
- In their attitude to homosexual activity?
- Any other?

Do They Know Whose Side You're On?

Joseph of Arimathea was a member of the Jewish council. It was an important group of men; they had the authority over the country's religious decisions. But there was an increasing anti-Jesus of Nazareth sentiment on the council, and it was becoming increasingly vocal as Jesus became more famous and more popular. Joseph had seen and heard for Himself what Jesus was doing and saying. He had decided that He was in fact genuine, and so he had decided to follow Him. But he hadn't told anyone about it. The others assumed he was in agreement with their opposition to Jesus, because he never spoke up.

But now things were heating up. The council was becoming very worried that their position was being threatened by Jesus' teaching, and they were talking about taking drastic action to get rid of Him. Joseph realized that he was coming to a decision point. He couldn't go along with it. But they didn't know he was secretly a disciple of Jesus. Things would get very nasty when they found out. And it would most definitely be a career-ending move. What would you have done?

It was the cross that was the turning point. Christ's crucifixion brought Joseph out into the open to declare where he stood: *"After this, Joseph of Arimathea, being a disciple of Jesus, but secretly for fear of the Jews, asked Pilate that he might take away the body of Jesus; and Pilate gave him permission. So he came and took the body of Jesus"* (John 19:38). Do they know whose side you're on?

Presenting Your Members

Your "members" referred to in Romans 6 are your body parts. Paul is telling you not to allow your body to be used for "unrighteous" activities, but to offer them to be used for "righteous" activities. Again, notice that it is very active on your part. Christ has conquered the power of sin within you so that it cannot force you to sin. It therefore requires conscious decisions on your part to take control of your body to *"... present your bodies a living sacrifice, holy acceptable to God, which is your reasonable service ..."* (Romans 12:1), because *"... if by the Spirit you put to death the deeds of the body you will live ..."* (Romans 8:13).

Paul said, "*... I discipline my body and bring it into subjection ...*" (1 Corinthians 9:27) and he did so because, as he stated, "*... your body is the temple of the Holy Spirit who is in you, whom you have from God, and you are not your own ...*" (1 Corinthians 6:19-20). This is why we he said we should "*... glorify God in your body and in your spirit, which are God's ...*" (1 Corinthians 6:20).

Depriving yourself of things that are naturally gratifying to your body but which are harmful spiritually involves self-denial, which is an integral part of discipleship. It is the "discipline" of discipleship. The Lord Jesus said: "*If anyone desires to come after Me, let him deny himself, and take up his cross daily and follow Me. For whoever desires to save his life will lose it, but whoever loses his life for My sake will save it. For what advantage is it to a man if he gains the whole world, and is himself destroyed or lost?*" (Luke 9:23-25).

What are examples from your own life of things that the members of your body should and should not be doing because you are dead to sin and alive to God?

- Things your eyes should not see (e.g. Matt.26:41; Matt.5:28; 1 John 2:16) and things they should see;
- Things your **ears** should not hear (e.g. Rom.10:17; Rev.2:7; Mark 4:24) and things they should hear;
- Things your **mouth** should not say (e.g. Eph.4:25,29; Eph.5:12,19,20; James 5:9-16) and things it should say;
- Things your **hands** should not do (e.g. Eph.4:28; James 1:23; 4:8; Col.2:21; 1 Cor.7:1) and things they should do;
- Places your **feet** should not go (e.g. Matt.28:19; Eph.6:15; James 1:27; 2 Thess.2:14) and places they should go

What do 1 Thessalonians 4:3–5; Ephesians 5:3; Ephesians 5:18 teach on this?

Going Deeper – A Self-Evaluation

Here is a self-evaluation. Score yourself on the following 3 questions: ("2" for "it's frequently true'; "1" for "it's occasionally true"; and "0" for "it's seldom or never true".)

1. I am aware of personal tendencies within me to be proud, or greedy, or selfish.
2. I am aware of an inner struggle between gratifying my natural inclinations and obeying the mind of the Lord.
3. I long to have a deeper, more consistent relationship with the Lord and sense of His presence.

How did you rate yourself out of a score of 6? What would you like your score to be?

Is the cross of Christ an offence to you? Or have you decided once and for all that you intend to live God's way, by His power, and not your own way, in your power? Have you realized that you can't have "the best of both worlds"? Are you "going deeper"?

2

Module 2 - Life to the Full

"I have come that they might have life, and might have it more abundantly." (John 10:10)

From Death to Life

In module 1 we looked at the practical reality of the spiritual fact that we "died to sin." This time we are going to examine the other side of it - that we are now "alive to Christ.' And so the two sides are: "dead to sin" and "alive to God." *"You also, reckon yourselves to be dead indeed to sin, but alive to God in Christ Jesus our Lord"* (Romans 6:11).

We also learned about what we are - that we are "sinners" - and how the cross of Christ is applicable every day as we put to death the natural deeds of our bodies. In this module, we are going to explore the other side - which is the essence of the eternal life that we received at the moment of our salvation. We will see that at its heart it involves the "knowledge" of God. And so again the two sides are: "knowing ourselves" and "knowing God."

What Exactly is Eternal Life?

At your salvation you received the gift of God - eternal life: *"the gift of God is eternal life in Christ Jesus our Lord"* (Romans 6:23). We know that eternal life is "everlasting" - it will never end. But is there any more to it than that? And when does it begin? Eternal life is the life that God Himself has, and was shown in person in Christ coming to this earth: *"the life was manifested, and we have seen, and bear witness, and declare to you that eternal life which was with the Father and was manifested to us"* (1 John 1:2).

We don't have to wait until Christ returns for us to have this life or to begin to enjoy it. We received it at the moment of our salvation and the means have been provided for us to live it right now:

"These things I have written to you who believe in the name of the Son of God, that you may know that you have eternal life" (1 John 5:13).

"I have come that they may have life, and that they may have it more abundantly" (John 10:10).

The essence of eternal life is "knowing God," Jesus said: *"this is eternal life, that they may know You, the only true God, and Jesus Christ whom You have sent"* (John 17:3). When the Bible talks about knowing God, it doesn't just mean knowing about God. It means understanding Him and having a relationship with Him. It means "experiencing" God. To illustrate this, the Bible refers to a husband and wife's intimate relationship with each other as "knowing" each other. An example of this is Joseph and Mary in Matthew 1:25.

Checkpoint – Eternal Life is for Now

```
Eternal life is a life of unlimited quantity ... and
a life of unlimited quality. To what extent are you
living in the enjoyment of this life right now?
```

There are stages in our increasing knowledge of God – degrees of "going deeper"- for example:

1. Knowing that there is a God
2. Knowing God personally, and His Son, Jesus Christ
3. Knowing the power of Christ in your daily life
4. Having "the unity of the faith" and the of knowledge of the Son of God"

Knowing That There Is a God

When the young man David went out after Goliath of the Philistines with just a slingshot, he said that he would defeat him for the purpose: *"that all the earth may know that there is a God in Israel"* (1 Samuel 17:46). David had a testimony for the God of Israel to the Philistines, for their judgment.

Checkpoint – Reflecting God to Others

People are first likely to come to know about the
reality of God by what they see of Him in your life.
In what ways are people around you convinced about
God by what they see in your faith?

When God was sending Moses to speak to Pharaoh to let the
people go, He said to him *"See, I have made you as God to Pharaoh"*
(Exodus 7:1). This knowledge that there is a God can only occur
by revelation of God's Holy Spirit. This is the first level of divine
revelation – that God exists, that He is unique (see 2 Kings 5:15)
and that He is the creator of all things. Many people in the world
deny this fact, and substitute other theories, but God's basic
expectation of every human being is that they acknowledge His
existence as their creator:

*"without faith it is impossible to please Him, for he who comes to
God must believe that He is, and that He is a rewarder of those who
diligently seek Him"* (Hebrews 11:6).

*"since the creation of the world His invisible attributes are clearly
seen, being understood by the things that are made, even His
eternal power and Godhead, so that they are without excuse ..."*
(Romans 1:20).

Checkpoint - Is there a God?

Do you ever doubt the existence of God? What causes
you to have these doubts? What are the things that

particularly give you assurance that God is God?

Knowing God and His Son, Jesus Christ

Knowing that there is a God should lead people to seek to know Him personally. Many people express a vague belief in God but are very unaware of just who He is and what He's like. Knowing God personally can only be done through a knowledge of God's Son; there is no other way:

"this is eternal life, that they may know You, the only true God, and Jesus Christ whom You have sent" (John 17:3).

"we know that the Son of God has come and has given us an understanding, that we may know Him who is true; and we are in Him who is true, in His Son Jesus Christ. This is the true God and eternal life" (1 John 5:20).

Many people and many religions proclaim that they believe in God, but they do not necessarily believe in His Son. And yet this is absolutely necessary. Jesus said: *"you believe in God, believe also in Me"* (John 14.1). He made it clear that belief in Him was the key to their salvation:

"Jesus said to him, 'I am the way, the truth, and the life; no one comes to the Father except through Me. If you had known Me, you would have known My Father also; and from now on you know Him and have seen Him" (John 14:6-7).

"therefore I said to you that you will die in your sins; for if you do not believe that/am He, you will die in your sins" (John 8:24).

When you share your faith with other people (such as by telling them about answered prayer), it is important to talk to them about the Lord Jesus Christ, as well as about God in general.

Knowing the Power of Christ

Once you come to know Jesus Christ as your Saviour and Lord at your salvation, it is possible to go deeper still and begin to experience what the apostle Paul referred to as *"the excellence of the knowledge of Christ Jesus my Lord"* (Philippians 3:8). This excellence was something Paul aspired to constantly in His life as a disciple. He describes it in verses 8 to 14 of Philippians chapter 3.

Paraphrase in your own words what you think he meant by the following expressions:

1. *"I count all things to be loss in view of the surpassing value of knowing Christ Jesus my Lord, for whom I have suffered the loss of all things, and count them but rubbish ..."*
2. *"... that I may know Him and the power of His resurrection..."*
3. *"... and the fellowship of His sufferings, being conformed to His death; in order that I may attain to the resurrection from the dead."*
4. *"...Not that I have already obtained it or have already become perfect, but I press on so that I may lay hold of that for which also I was laid hold of by Christ Jesus. Brethren, I do not regard myself as having laid hold of it yet; but one thing I do: forgetting*

what lies behind and reaching forward to what lies ahead, I press on toward the goal for the prize of the upward call of God in Christ Jesus."

What did Paul mean by "the power of His resurrection"? It is the power that accomplished Christ's resurrection and gave Him an indissoluble life — that is the Holy Spirit:

"that you may know... what is the exceeding greatness of His power towards us who believe, according to the working of His mighty power which He worked in Christ when He raised Him from the dead" (Ephesians 1:18-20).

"Jesus Christ our Lord, who was... declared to be the Son of God with power according to the Spirit of holiness, by the resurrection from the dead" (Romans 1:3,4).

We know, as believers in Christ, that the Spirit of God is in us bodily and will never leave us (1 Corinthians 6:19; Ephesians 1:13,14). However, His presence and power may not always be very strong or evident in our lives. It is an amazing fact that He will only exert His unlimited power in us with our active consent. The Bible says that He "yearns" inside us (James 4:5).

Checkpoint - God's Power in Your Life

```
Do you have a similar longing for Him - that you
would more consistently allow His power to work in
your life? Have you learned to conduct your life in
the same power by which you initially received
```

eternal life - the power of the Spirit of God?
"Having begun in the Spirit, are you now being made
perfect by the flesh?" (Galatians 3:3).

The Lord Jesus intends that our lives for Him on this earth be satisfying and fulfilling life, even though it may entail hardships. He referred to it as His "joy" and He was describing being committed to a purpose that gave everything proper meaning:

"These things I have spoken to you, that My joy may remain in you, and that your joy may be full" (John 15:11).

"Therefore you now have sorrow; but I will see you again and your heart will rejoice, and your joy no one will take from you" (John 16:22).

"Until now you have asked nothing in My name. Ask, and you will receive, that your joy may be full" (John 16:24).

"But now I come to You, and these things I speak in the world, that they may have My joy fulfilled in themselves" (John 17:13).

It is vital that you develop and sustain the daily habits of "living life to the full". They are "the discipline of discipleship." Here is a self-test you can apply. Score yourself on the following questions: "2" if it's frequently true, "1" if it's only occasionally true, and "0" if it's seldom or never true.

1. I enjoy sitting down and reading the Bible for myself.
2. Praying about something that concerns me is usually one

of the first things that I do about it.

3. When I read the Bible I find it meaningful to me.

4. I can readily unburden myself to the Lord about things that concern me, both about myself and others.

5. When I learn something from the scriptures that I should or should not do, I feel a need to put it into practice.

6. After praying earnestly about a decision, and waiting on the Lord, I feel a peace about it.

7. When I discover something new about the Lord Jesus, I tell His Father about it and what I appreciate about it.

How did you score, out of a maximum possible of 14? What did you learn about yourself from trying to answer the questions?

The power of the Holy Spirit in your life will be directly proportional to the degree to which you:

- continually surrender your will to His will (as we saw in Module 1);
- put sin away from your life, recognizing it and confessing it promptly when it occurs (as we'll see in Module 3);
- are continually "feeding on the Word of God, by reading, studying and reflecting on the Bible;
- are consistently being obedient to what the Spirit of God shows you from His Word; and
- are in regular communion with God in prayer and worship.

Checkpoint - Groups

Many people find it helpful to belong to a small
group that meets regularly in a home for Bible study,
prayer, sharing their experiences and discussing the
work of the Lord. Do you belong to such a group?
Would you like to? (If so, let one of the leaders in
your church know).

Having the Unity of the Faith and of the Knowledge of the Son of God

No matter how deep we progress in our individual knowledge
and experience with God, there is much more. God has also
saved us to bring us all into a complete unity with Him, and
therefore with each other. This unity has three aspects to it:

a) **The unity of our "common salvation'** (Jude 3) whereby we
are all unconditionally members of Christ's body, with Him as
its head.

- *"There is one body and one Spirit, just as you were called/n one
  hope of your calling"* (Ephesians 4:4,5).
- *"For as the body is one and has many members, but all the
  members of that one body being many, are one body, so also is
  Christ"* (1 Corinthians 12:12).

b) **The unity of 'the faith"** which includes all the teachings of
Christ, which He has passed on through His apostles - "the
apostles' teaching" (Acts 2:42) that disciples are to continue
steadfastly in:

- *"There is ... one Lord, **one faith** ..."* (Ephesians 4:5).
- *"Examine yourselves as to whether you are in **the faith**. Prove yourselves ..."* (2 Corinthians 13:5).
- *"... wage the good warfare, having faith and a good conscience, which some having rejected concerning **the faith** have suffered shipwreck"* (1 Timothy 1:18,19).
- *"I have fought the good fight, I have finished the race, I have kept **the faith**"* (2 Timothy 4:7).

c) **The unity of being at peace and unity of mind with others**, through the work of the Holy Spirit.

- *"endeavouring to keep the unity of the Spirit in the bond of peace"* (Ephesians 4:3).
- *"I plead with you, brethren, by the name of our Lord Jesus Christ, that you all speak the same thing, and that there be no divisions among you, but that you be perfectly joined together in the same mind and in the same judgment"* (1 Corinthians 1:10).

Checkpoint - Am I United with God?

```
The Body - Am I a member of the church the body of
Christ through personal salvation?
The Faith - Am I continuing steadfastly in the Lord's
teaching together with other baptised disciples in
churches of God?
My Mind - Am I living in harmony with other saints in
my assembly? Are there any exceptions?
```

In the book of Ephesians, the apostle Paul goes into some

detail about "the church the body of Christ' - that relationship between all believers and Christ. In chapter 4 he goes on to describe how living members of that body could aspire to function as an integrated whole, as a full- grown person. He explains this in verses 11 to 13:

"... He Himself gave some to be apostles, some prophets, some evangelists, and some pastors and teachers, for the equipping of the saints for the work of ministry ..."

The early apostles (like Paul) and other men were given as gifts to the saints in the churches of God to equip them to minister (to serve together). Apostles and New Testament prophets laid down the foundation teaching (Ephesians 2:20; 1 Corinthians 3:10,11; Acts 2:42). Evangelists spread it to others. Teachers taught it. And pastors cared for those who had been taught.

"... for the edifying of the body of Christ ..."

The ministering of the saints was for the purpose of strength-ening and building up the body of believers in the teaching of Christ. But what was the end objective of that upbuilding?

"... till we all come to the unity of the faith and of the knowledge of the Son of God ..."

The objective was the unity in practice of all the believers in ad-herence to the teaching of Christ and to a collective relationship with Him in all His functions.

"... to a perfect (complete) man, to the measure of the stature of the

fullness of Christ."

This desired end-state is the total united functioning of living members of the body of Christ, like a single person and not disjointed parts. The complete man is not you as an individual believer but all believers in total.

Checkpoint – Connecting the Body parts

> If the key to coming to "the unity of the faith and of the knowledge of the Son of God" is adhering jointly to all the teaching of Christ as revealed in scripture, why is the Christian world so divided and fragmented today? What does this scripture tell us is God's remedy for this situation? What part does He want you to play in helping to achieve this?

And so the full knowledge of Christ is more than an individual experience. It involves being joined together with other obedient disciples according to "the faith" to function as the house of God, the place where God wants to be served collectively. For example, to experience a relationship with Jesus Christ as your Saviour (Philippians 3:20) is an individual experience. But to experience Him as your High Priest (Hebrews 10:21) requires being part of the people of God in the house of God.

What other functions that Christ performs today in heaven can be experienced individually, and which require being part of the people of God in churches of God? For example:

- "Good Shepherd" (John 10:11)
- "Great Shepherd" (1 Peter 5:1-4)
- "Advocate (Counselor)" (1 John 2:1)
- "High Priest" (Hebrews 4:15)
- Mediator of the new covenant (Hebrews 8:6-10)

"The ignorance of God - both of His ways and of the practice of communion with Him - lies at the root of much of the church's weakness today" (J.I. Packer). Could that be said of you or your church?

Going Deeper

Which do you think is more important - your personal communion with God, or your service for God? The answer, without question, is that they are equally important because they are inseparable and mutually dependent. Living "abundant life" through the power of the Holy Spirit inside you will inevitably cause you to want to serve God in an acceptable way to Him. Trying to serve God without His power inside being reflected in your life will be mechanical, empty and fruitless. Going deeper in your knowledge and relationship with God, and His Son Jesus Christ your Lord, through the power of the Holy Spirit, therefore involves engaging in service for God - in two directions:

- **To God** - Worship, praise and prayer to God (both individually and jointly in churches of God); and
- **For God** - Serving others in the churches and elsewhere with whichever ministries the Holy Spirit has gifted you.

A Self-assessment

To what extent do you contribute to your church by living and serving God acceptably in the following ways? (Rate yourself on a scale of 1 to 10 on each question.)

1. We regularly offer fresh rich appreciation to God for His Son in our worship.
2. We continually gather together and support each other in relying on the Lord in prayer.
3. We continually seek to learn more of the Lord's teaching for our lives and work for Him.
4. We continually strive to avoid sin and worldliness to be clean to serve the Lord.
5. We regularly encourage each other to develop our God-given gift and to fulfill our ministry in harmony together.
6. We constantly work to develop stronger relationships with each other, while excluding no one.
7. We consistently and effectively reach out to our communities outside to evangelize and to meet their needs.
8. We are sensitive to each other's needs, and strive to show our love to them in practical ways.
9. We know and value what it means to be a church of God, in the house of God and in the Fellowship of God's Son.
10. We are known by others as people who love each other, and who also show their love for other people by doing good works for them.

What was your score out of 100? Where do you think you need to focus your attention?

There is sometimes a tendency to put blame on others if our church is not effective. However all we can control is ourselves, and we must take accountability for that. ***"If it's going to be, it has to be me."***

3

Module 3 - Pressing on to the Goal

"I press towards the goal for the prize of the upward call of God in Christ Jesus." (Philippians 3:14)

Setbacks

Once you have determined to set out in your discipleship life in God's strength and not your own, bowing completely to His will in everything (Module 1), and then to enter into the fullness of your eternal life through the power of the Spirit of God within you, whereby you develop a deeper and deeper relationship with God (Module 2), isn't that all there is to it? Sadly, you will quickly find that it's not as straight-forward as that. You will have setbacks and discouragements and difficulties. If you're not ready for them, and don't know how to deal with them when they suddenly arrive, you'll find the way hard and frustrating.

Our key text in Module 3 is Hebrews 12:1-17 where, after being shown in chapter 10 the wonderful privilege of our entrance into the very presence of God as a people in worship, and then being encouraged on in our faith to do exactly that by the large number of examples in chapter 11, we come to chapter 12, where it says:

"Therefore since we also are surrounded by so great a cloud of witnesses, let us lay aside every weight, and the sin which so easily ensnares us, and let us run with endurance the race that is set before us, looking unto Jesus, the author and finisher of our faith, who for the joy that was set before Him endured the cross, despising the shame, and has sat down at the right hand of the throne of God. For consider Him who endured such hostility from sinners against Himself, lest you become weary and discouraged in your souls. You have not yet resisted to bloodshed, striving against sin."

"And you have forgotten the exhortation which speaks to you as to sons: 'My son, do not despise the chastening of the LORD, nor be discouraged when you are rebuked by Him; For whom the LORD loves He chastens, and scourges every son whom He receives.' If you endure chastening, God deals with you as with sons; for what son is there whom a father does not chasten? But if you are without chastening, of which all have become partakers, then you are illegitimate and not sons. Furthermore, we have had human fathers who corrected us, and we paid them respect. Shall we not much more readily be in subject/on to the Father of spirits and live? For they indeed for a few days chastened us as seemed best to them, but He for our profit, that we may be partakers of His holiness. Now no chastening seems to be joyful for the present, but grievous; nevertheless, afterwards it yields the peaceable fruit of

righteousness to those who have been trained by it."

"Therefore strengthen the hands which hang down, and the feeble knees, and make straight paths for your feet, so that what is lame may not be dislocated, but rather be healed. Pursue peace with all men, and holiness, without which no one will see the Lord: looking diligently lest anyone fall short of the grace of God; lest any root of bitterness springing up should cause trouble, and by this many become defiled; lest there be any fornicator or profane person like Esau, who for one morsel of food sold his birthright. For you know that afterwards, when he wanted to inherit the blessing, he was rejected, for he found no place for repentance, though he sought it diligently with tears" (Hebrews 12:1-17).

Discouragement - How to Survive the Spiritual "Lows"

This passage acknowledges that discouragement is very possible in Christian life. It doesn't mean that you are a poor Christian if you become discouraged from time to time. Here are two illustrations from the Old Testament:

- David as a young man, even though he knew he had been chosen by God to be king one day, became very discouraged at the persecution by King Saul. One day his good friend came to his aid: *"Then Jonathan, Saul's son, arose and went to David in the woods and strengthened his hand in God"'*(1 Samuel 23:16).
- The great prophet Elijah, despite his miraculous victories over King Ahab, Jezebel and the prophets of the idol Baal,

became very discouraged because he thought he was the only faithful one left. He said: *"I have been very zealous for the LORD God of hosts; for the children of Israel have forsaken Your covenant, torn down Your altars, and killed Your prophets with the sword. I alone am left; and they seek to take my life"* (1 Kings 19:10). The Lord reassured him with the answer: *"I have reserved seven thousand in Israel, all whose knees have not bowed to Baal"* (1 Kings 19:18).

Checkpoint – Do You get Discouraged?

```
To what extent are you discouraged from time to time
with: being in a small church; lack of good Christian
friends: the lifestyle of some other young people in
your church; your inconsistency in daily quiet times
with the Lord; your inhibitions about witnessing;
your tendency to certain bad habits; the rat race,
etc.
```

Discouragement can result from several possible causes. such as:

- Opposition from other people (such as David experienced)
- A feeling of weakness or of being all alone (such as Elijah experienced)
- A feeling of failure (such as Peter experienced, after he had denied the Lord - Matthew 26:75)
- A feeling that the way is too [raid to keep going (such as John Mark experienced, when he went home from traveling with Paul and Barnabas on their missionary journey - Acts 15:38)

Hebrews 12 gives you the remedy when discouragement strikes:

1. You are to focus on the Lord Jesus and how lie endured despite the opposition He was exposed to. He finished His race, and that can encourage you to finish your race too. It is a marathon, not a sprint, and so you need patience and endurance just when it seems the hardest. He resisted to the extent of bloodshed; you are unlikely to be called to do that, these verses say.

2. You are to realize that the difficulty might be due to the fact that God wants to teach you something, that it's part of His discipline as your Father (there's more on this below).

3. You are to realize that one purpose of it may be to make you sensitive to when others are going through similar discouraging times, so that you will be able to help them with real empathy: *"Blessed be the God and Father of out Lord Jesus Christ, the Father of mercies and God of all comfort, who comforts us in all our tribulation, that we may be able to comfort those who are in any trouble. with the comfort with which we ourselves are comforted by God. For as the sufferings of Christ abound in us, so our consolation also abounds through Christ"* (2 Corinthians 1:3-5).

Checkpoint - Discouragement

How can your church be an effective support group to you when you are going through spiritually discouraging times? Are you willing to let them support you in those times, or do you withdraw from them? Are you alert and ready to do the same for

```
others in your church?
```

A lovely case study of this kind of support is how the Lord helped those two people who were walking to Emmaus from Jerusalem on the Sunday night of His resurrection (refer to Luke 24:13-35):

- What mood were they in on that occasion, and why?
- How did Jesus approach them in such a way to get them to open up to Him?
- How did He enable them to overcome their discouragement?
- In what ways was their return trip to Jerusalem that night different from the trip to Emmaus?
- What practical lessons can you learn from this episode?
- How does this illustrate the Lord's functioning as a "counselor"?

God's Discipline

One of the ways that God shows His love to you is to discipline you. This may sound contradictory until you realize that this is the same way that a good father brings up his children when they need correction. It reminds you that, not only are you His children because of the new birth at salvation, but He takes a continuing interest in you as His sons and daughters (2 Corinthians 6:18; that is He cares how you "turn out" - how you develop and mature).

God's disciplinary action is therefore proof that you are in fact His sons (and daughters) and that He loves you. You therefore need to submit yourself to this discipline and not push back at it.

(Remember what the Lord said to Saul of Tarsus when he was on the way to Damascus: *"It is hard for you to kick against the goads"* (Acts 9:5); Saul had been resisting the Lord's work in his heart.

God's discipline results in your improvement and aligns you with what He wants you to be - it makes you a "partaker of His holiness." That is, you increasingly share in the things that belong solely to Him. There is an important distinction between God's discipline of you as His son or daughter, and His judgment on people in the world for their wrongdoing. His motive is entirely different: *"when we are judged, we are chastened by the Lord, that we may not be condemned with the world"* (1 Corinthians 11:32).

The previous verse to this also shows you how we can limit the discipline that God needs to put us through: *"if we would judge ourselves, we would not be judged"* (1 Corinthians 11:31). That is, to the extent that you continually examine yourself by God's Word and change the things that need to change, the less painful will be the process of God accomplishing what He wants in you.

Why Do Godly People Suffer?

This is a very common question that is often asked. Suffering is not usually, as some people might think, a punishment; it is a means God uses to refine us, to change us, to bring us into a deeper experience with Him. For example, in the upper room, Christ referred to His disciples as branches of the vine (John 15:1,2), and said that those branches which bear fruit will be pruned by His Father: *"that it might bear more fruit."* (Branches that don't bear any fruit will be destroyed, He said.) This pruning process can be painful.

The best insight into the meaning of suffering is the case study of Lord Jesus Himself. Hebrews chapter 2 describes to us why it was necessary for Christ as a man to suffer. It certainly wasn't because of sin or the need to improve, in His case: *"For it was fitting for Him, for whom are all things and by whom are all things, in bringing many sons to glory to make the author of their salvation perfect through sufferings"* (Hebrews 2:10). Christ had to firstly undergo the suffering of temptation (verse 18) and then the suffering of death (verse 9) so as to be complete ("perfect') in His experience, so as to be equipped to become our intercessory high priest in heaven today. Suffering is a prerequisite to completeness. The process is the same for us.

Scripture seems to refer to three different kinds of suffering. Perhaps you have been exposed to one or more of these:

1. The first of these is religious persecution - "suffering as a Christian." It may just be a mild form of ridicule or ostracism, or it might be more severe. Peter talked about it in his first epistle and encouraged the believers to persevere through it: *"if anyone suffers as a Christian, let him not be ashamed, but let him glorify God in this matter"* (1 Peter 4:16).

2. The second form of suffering is affliction of various kinds - poor health, bereavement, loneliness, unemployment, relationship problems, and many more - which can severely try your faith. "Trying' your faith is, literally, proving or testing your faith, and it is also intended to have the effect of "im-proving" your faith. Peter refers to this as follows: *"In this you greatly rejoice, though now for a little*

while, if need be, you have been grieved by various trials, that the genuineness of your faith, being much more precious than gold that perishes though it is tested by fire, may be found to praise. honour; and glory at the revelation of Jesus Christ" (1 Peter 1:6,7). Amazingly, James actually said we are to be happy when this happens to us: *"My brethren, count it all joy when you fall into various trials, knowing that the testing of your faith produces patience"* (James 1:2,3).

3. There is a third form of suffering - enduring temptation. This is the struggle between our old and our new natures. James refers to this in his epistle: *"Blessed is the man who endures temptation; for when he has been proved, he will receive the crown of life which the Lord has promised to those who love Him"* (James 1:12).

Checkpoint — Suffering

```
Is there a way in which you have been or are
suffering? Have you thought about it in terms of it
being part of God's means of drawing you closer to
Him? Do you think that better understanding the
purpose for what you are going through will help you
to endure it, and even to welcome it?
```

James goes on to describe the process by which temptation works in you. He describes it as though it were a birth - in four stages: *'But each one is tempted when he is drawn away by his own desires and enticed. Then, when desire has conceived, it gives birth to sin; and sin, when it is full-grown, brings forth death"* (James 1:14-15).

1. **Attraction** - The first step is the union between some outside attraction and the inner urge which is part of your "old man." You cannot prevent the attraction coming into your mind through your senses, such as your eyesight or your hearing. But you can prevent it, by the Holy Spirit's power, from uniting with your inner craving (your "desires"), and so 'conceiving" sin - which is something that takes place in your mind.

2. **Conception** – The second step is you allowing your desire for the attraction to be gratified. This may be so "second nature" to you in some cases that it is hardly conscious.

3. **Birth** - This is the action that results from the thought - the actual committing of the wrong-doing.

4. **Death** - If the sin is allowed to foster and develop unchecked, it will suffocate and neutralize your spiritual life - the abundant life of the Holy Spirit within you. (Sin is like a dangerous animal in your life. When a lion is small it looks attractive and harmless. But allowed to grow unchecked, it will do what it is equipped to do, and that is destroy. "Little lions become big lions, and big lions kill. Little sins become big sins and big sins kill."

The Case of Judas Iscariot

Like you, Judas was a disciple of the Lord Jesus. But he committed an extremely serious and damaging sin from which he never recovered. It prevented him from being one of the twelve apostles who would be the core of the Lord's work from the time of Pentecost on. What happened? Let's analyze his experience using the 4 steps above:

1. **Attraction** - Judas' particular weakness (his "lust") was greed for money: *"... he was a thief, and had the money box; and he used to take what was put in it"* (John 12:6). This was combined with an opportunity to earn a reward from betraying Jesus, because he knew the Jewish leaders were looking for a way to get rid of Him.

2. **Conception** - Instead of dismissing the idea immediately, Judas pondered it. We know that this thought originated with Satan: *"the devil having already put it into the heart of Judas Iscariot, Simon's son, to betray Him"* (John 13:2).

3. **Birth** - What prompted him to act ("the trigger') was his displeasure at the Lord rebuking him for how he had treated Mary. He immediately went to see the chief priests (John 12:4-8; Matthew 26:1- 16 - *"What are you willing to give me if I deliver Him to you? And they counted out to him thirty pieces of silver. So from that time he sought opportunity to betray Him."* His opportunity came in the garden of Gethsemane, where he knew Jesus would be that night (John 18:2). He led the posse to the garden and identified Jesus by kissing Him: *"Jesus said to him, Judas, are you betraying the Son of Man with a kiss?"* (Luke 22:48).

4. **Death** - While Judas realized what he had done and returned the money, he was not given repentance. His sin destroyed him: *"Then he threw down the pieces of silver in the temple and departed, and went and hanged himself"* Matthew 27:5.

Do you see any lessons in this for yourself?

As a follower of Jesus Christ you are expected by Him to avoid all forms of sin at all costs. Sin is deadly. Tolerating it, or worse, enjoying it, is a sure way to destroy your spiritual life. John said in his first epistle: *"My little children, these things I write to you, so that you may not sin"* (1 John 2:1), while the apostle said we should live *"… as free, yet not using liberty as a cloak for vice, but as bondservants of God"* (1 Peter 2:16).

Whenever temptation is at work in your life, there is always another counter-acting force at work. You should never blame God for tempting you to sin; He does not do that. Satan tempts. What God always does, simultaneously, is to make a way for you to escape the temptation:

"No temptation has overtaken you except such as is common to man; but God is faithful, who will not allow you to be tempted beyond what you are able. but with the temptation will also make the way of escape, that you may be able to bear it" (1 Corinthians 10:13).

"Let no one say when he is tempted, 'I am tempted by God'; for God cannot be tempted by evil, nor does He Himself tempt anyone. But each one is tempted when he is drawn away by his own desires and enticed" (James 1:13-14).

All sin starts in your mind - in the attraction and conception stages. Therefore the key to preventing sin is controlling you is when it first enters your thoughts. Consciously put it out of your mind, praying and asking God to help you do that. Do not give it an inch or else it will allow Satan to build a stronghold in your mind. This is what Paul talked about: *"For the weapons of our warfare are not carnal but mighty in God for pulling down strongholds, casting down arguments and every high thing that exalts itself against the knowledge of God, bringing every thought into captivity to the obedience of Christ, and being ready to punish all disobedience when your obedience is fulfilled"* (2 Corinthians 10:4-6).

These are extremely important and powerful verses. (The seven "weapons of your warfare" are identified in Ephesians 6:13-18.) Of course, if you are going to recognize sin when you are being tempted, you will have to know what God's standard of "right" is. This can only be the case to the extent you are regularly finding it out from reading His Word:

- *"the word of the LORD is right, and all His work is done in truth"* (Psalm 33:4).
- *"Your word I have hidden in my heart, that I might not sin against You!"* (Psalm 119:11).

Checkpoint — Avoiding Sin "Like the Plague"

- What are the 7 weapons? Explain them in your own words and how using them allows you to prevent sin from damaging your life for God.
- What does "bringing every thought into captivity to the obedience of Christ" mean to you?
- What does "being ready to punish all disobedience when your obedience is fulfilled" mean to you?
- Do you look for God's "way of escape" when you realize you are being tempted?
- Are there any things that you have learned recently from the Bible that are sin, that you didn't previously think were wrong?

The Road to Recovery

But we all do sin, and can't expect to become totally sinless in this lifetime: *"If we say that we have no sin, we deceive ourselves, and the truth is not in us"* (1 John 1:8). And so what do you do? How do you avoid it destroying your life and usefulness for God, and your full enjoyment of "the abundant life"? Let's look at 4 milestones on the road to recovery:

1) **Conviction** - Realizing that something you have done is wrong is a work of the Holy Spirit in your conscience. It affects your mind (understanding that if is contrary to God's way) and also your heart (being sorry about it and wishing you hadn't done it) This work of God is what leads to repentance (changing your direction).

- *"He will convict the world of sin, and of righteousness, and of judgment of sin, because they do riot believe in Me"* (John 16:8,9).
- *"... in humility correcting those who are in opposition, ii perhaps God will grant them repentance, so that they may know the truth"* (2 Timothy 2:25).
- *"... godly sorrow produces repentance leading to salvation, not to be regretted; but the sorrow of the world produces death"* (2 Corinthians 7:10).

2) **Confession** - Often the hardest thing for anyone to do is to admit that they were wrong. But it is vital to recovery You must admit your sin: (1) to yourself; (2) to God; and (3) to the person you have sinned against (if this is the case):

- *"If we confess our sins, He is faithful and just to forgive us our sins and to cleanse us from all unrighteousness"* (1 John 1:9).
- *"Confess your trespasses to one another; and pray for one another; that you may be healed. The effective, fervent prayer of a righteous man avails much"* (James 5:16).

How is this triple confession shown in the case of the prodigal son in Luke chapter 15? *"But when he came to himself, he said, 'How many of my fathers hired servants have bread enough and to spare, and I perish with hunger! I will arise and go to my father; and will say to him, Father I have sinned against heaven and before you"* (Luke 15:17-18).

3) Correction - If your sin is ongoing, you obviously need to stop it. If it has affected someone else, you need to sincerely apologize and to make amends for whatever damage has been done. Hopefully, they will forgive you but you can't control that. If you have done what you need to do, you are clear; if they refuse to forgive you, that is their problem, and it will be damaging to them. Often a certain amount of time is needed for someone to get over it even if they have said they accept your apology and have forgiven you.

As Christians we are required to forgive one another. If Christ, who in His sinlessness never needed to be forgiven by anyone for anything, has forgiven you for the sin which took Him to Calvary, is there anything at all for which you should not forgive someone else? *"... be kind to one another tenderhearted, forgiving one another just as God in Christ also forgave you"* (Ephesians 4:32).

In Old Testament times, an Israelite was expected to repay a trespass plus 20%: *"And he shall make restitution for the harm that he has done in regard to the holy thing, and shall add one-fifth to it"* (Leviticus 5:16). Are there situations today where you do something against another person, where you should go beyond compensating them for whatever harm you have done?

4) Restoration - The first three steps are designed to bring you to the point of restoration of fellowship. Having purged yourself of your sin and cleansed your conscience, fellowship can now be restored firstly with God (who has been offended), and then with whoever else has been offended. If the sin involved disciplining a saint in the assembly, such as them having to be put away to avoid contaminating the church, restoration to fellowship is now possible. Without full restoration in these aspects the recovery process is not complete.

This is illustrated in the case of the man who had to be put away from the church of God in Corinth due to immorality (1 Corinthians 5). In 2 Corinthians, it seems clear that the man had been convicted of his sin in his own heart. He had repented and corrected it. And so Paul wrote to the church instructing them to receive him back into their fellowship: *"This punishment which was inflicted by the majority is sufficient for such a man, so that, on the contrary, you ought rather to forgive and comfort him, lest perhaps such a one be swallowed up with too much sorrow. Therefore I urge you to reaffirm your love to him"* (2 Corinthians 2:6-8).

The Case of Peter

If you think back to Peter, he as well as Judas committed a great sin at a crucial time by denying Christ. Peter recovered from it and went on to become a powerful leader for Christ. Let's examine how he went through the four milestones on the road to recovery:

1. **Conviction** – *"Peter remembered the word of Jesus who had said to him "Before the cock crows, you will deny Me three times.' So he went out and wept bitterly"* (Matthew 26:75).

2. **Confession** - We know from the Lord's words beforehand that Peter would repent; the Lord Himself was praying for this: *"... the Lord said, Simon, Simon! Indeed, Satan has asked for you, that he may sift you as wheat. But I have prayed for you, that your faith should not fail; and when you have returned to Me, strengthen your brethren"* (Luke 22:31–32).

3. **Correction** - Peter not only stopped denying the Lord, he became an outspoken witness for Him: *"Then Peter; filled with the Holy Spirit, said to them. 'Rulers of the people and elders of Israel ...'"* (Acts 4:8).

4. **Restoration** - Peter and the Lord came back into full fellowship with each other on the beach at Galilee after Jesus' resurrection, after the Lord had made a special meeting with him before appearing to the other apostles (see Luke 24:34; 1 Corinthians 15:5). *"Jesus said to Simon Peter; Simon, son of Jonah, do you love Me more than these? He said to Him, Yes, Lord; You know that! love You. He said to him, Feed My lambs ... when He had spoken this, He said to him, Follow Me"* (John 21:15–19).

Are there any lessons in this for you?

Judas' example shows us the sad possibility that we can waste our spiritual life. Peter's example, however, shows us that recovery is always possible, no matter what we've done or how badly we've failed.

Going Deeper - By Persevering

We have studied various forms of difficulties that can be setbacks in our daily drive towards the prize that God holds out for us. We have looked at discouragement; God's discipline; suffering; and temptation and sin. The Christian life is not intended to be easy. Christ said: *"These things I have spoken to you, that in Me you may have peace. In the world you will have tribulation: but be of good cheer; I have overcome the world"* (John 16:33).

There isn't a Christian alive who isn't trying to deal with these setbacks (unless they are living a totally worldly life). As the cross of Christ has its effect on our lives, we will he called on to carry our own cross (as Roman prisoners were required to do on the way to being crucified. It was a public display of their rejection by society: *"then Jesus said to His disciples, 'If anyone desires to come after Me, let him deny himself, and take up Ins cross, and follow Me. For whoever desires to save his life will lose it, but whoever loses his life for My sake will find it'"* (Matthew 16:24-25).

As we all go through these trials together, how can we help each other in our church to use these experiences for what they are intended to do, to purify us and conform us to the purpose for which God is shaping us, so that they might be a source of joy and not of grief?

"... we also glory in tribulations, knowing that tribulation produces perseverance; and perseverance, character; and character; hope" (Romans 5:3-4).

4

Module 4 - Salt & Light

"You are the salt of the earth" ..."You are the light of the world."
(Matthew 5:13,14)

Discovery of Mission – Making God Known

Peter's encounter with the Lord on the sea of Galilee in Luke 5 resulted in him discovering that he had a mission in life beyond himself - that he was to be a conduit through which the Lord would reach others; he would become a "fisher of men."

The more you get to know God and to have a deeper personal con-viction of His ways and His truth, the more this will inevitably overflow into a desire to win others for Him also - you too will discover a sense of mission. For example John, the Lord's apostle, described the intimate relationship he'd had with the Lord during His lifetime; he wanted others to share it ...

"That which was from the beginning, which we have heard, which we have seen with our eyes, which we have

looked upon, and our hands have handled, concerning the Word of life— the life was manifested, and we have seen, and bear witness, and declare to you that eternal life which was with the Father and was manifested to us— that which we have seen and heard ...”

“... we declare to you, that you also may have fellowship with us; and truly our fellowship is with the Father and with His Son Jesus Christ. And these things we write to you that your joy may be full” (1 John 1:1-4).

The early disciples were so on fire for the Lord that they couldn't help talking about it to those around them: *“they spoke the word of God with boldness”*; *“those who were scattered went everywhere preaching the word”* (Acts 4:31; 8:4). It is God's method of growth and expansion to spread His word through existing disciples. Some are used to "sow" and some to "reap": *“He who continually goes forth weeping, bearing seed for sowing, shall doubtless come again with rejoicing, bringing his sheaves with him”* (Psalm 126:6); *“both he who sows and he who reaps may rejoice together”* (John 4:36). We are therefore "chosen vessels" for this purpose, just as the apostle Paul was: *“He is a chosen vessel of Mine to bear My name before Gentiles, kings, and the children of Israel”* (Acts 9:15).

Checkpoint - Your Mission

```
Do you think of yourself as a missionary? Where is
your particular mission field?
```

Salt – A Restraining Effect

'You are the salt of the earth; but if the salt loses its taste, how shall it be seasoned? It is then good for nothing but to be thrown out and trampled underfoot by men" (Matthew 5:13).

1. Do people act differently around you because they know your beliefs and your lifestyle?
2. Do they avoid taking the Lord's name in vain?
3. Do they refrain from telling inappropriate jokes?
4. What are some of the legitimate ways in which your life can appear different from that of unbelievers? For example:

- Your **ego** - do you like to take the credit for things, or to be seen as the expert on certain things?
- Your **ambition** - do they see you as someone who is aspiring for promotions and higher positions at work?
- Your **greed** - do they hear you talking about wanting a raise and wanting to accumulate wealth?
- Your **actions** toward others - do they see you being "political' or manipulative toward others in getting what you want?
- Your **honesty** - are you "transparent"? Do you always tell "the truth, the whole truth and nothing but the truth"?
- Your **integrity** - do you "walk the talk"? Is your word your bond? Do you have credibility?
- Your **fairness** - do you treat everyone equally and honourably?

If you do all these things consistently at work, college, etc., you will be seen as different from most other people. People may not say anything to you, but they will notice. And they will probably talk about it to others. You will have a testimony to the Lord before them by your conduct. You will be salt that hasn't lost its savour.

Various people may react to seeing these examples of your faith in action in a variety of ways. For example, they might be indifferent, or they might want to have what you have. They may even persecute you by speaking against you, ostracizing you, or dealing unfairly with you because they see your behaviour as a condemnation of themselves.

"Let your speech always be with grace, seasoned with salt, that you may know how you ought to answer each one" (Colossians 4:6).

"But sanctify the Lord God in your hearts, and always be ready to give a defense to everyone who asks you a reason for the hope that is in you, with meekness and fear; having a good conscience, that when they defame you as evildoers, those who revile your good conduct in Christ may be ashamed" (1 Peter 3:15-16).

Checkpoint – What are Your Experiences?

    - How different is your life from most people that
    you work with or go to school with?
    - Do most people treat the fact that you are a
    practicing Christian with indifference?
    - Have any of them indicated that they would like to
    have a faith like you have?
    - Have any of them persecuted you in any way?

Your Social Responsibility

"have no fellowship with the unfruitful works of darkness, but rather expose them" (Ephesians 5:11).

"They are not of the world, just as I am not of the world" (John 17:16).

The Christian is told to *"be subject to the governing authorities. For there is no authority except from God, and the authorities that exist are appointed by God."* (Romans 13:1) However when is 'civil disobedience' the proper response, considering that *"We ought to obey God rather than men"'*(Acts 5:29)?

It is not the job of the Christian to reform society (this world is doomed to judgment), but rather to win people for Christ out of the world. We are "ambassadors for Christ" in foreign territory. Since you are a citizen of heaven, have you renounced your citizenship to earth, or are you still a dual citizen, trying to be loyal to two opposing powers? When World War II started, there were many British subjects living in Germany. The outbreak of the war necessitated them declaring their loyalty to one side or the other. They could no longer accommodate both sides. We are at war now (Ephesians 6:12,13)!

Should you use the political process of a democratic country, using your natural citizenship rights (such as voting) to achieve your objectives? For example, in voting for political leaders, realizing that it is God who *"removes kings and raises up kings"* (Daniel 2:21)? Are there some circumstances where voting is appropriate and some where it is not?

Should you as an individual, or together with your assembly, register God's point of view with the authorities on important social issues? What are some current topics of public debate and proposed legislation where this might be done? How might this best be done? How does Ephesians 5:11 apply to this situation? (*"have no fellowship with the unfruitful works of darkness, but rather expose them."*)

How can your involvement in charitable activity lend credence to your beliefs or detract from your testimony? Matthew 5:16 says, *"Let your light so shine before men, that they may see your good works and glorify your Father in heaven"* (Matthew 5:16), whereas Jesus exposes the Pharisees because *"all their works they do to be seen by men"* (Matthew 23:5). Do you have any personal experiences of this? How can you be more active in good works, without compromising your separated position in the churches, so that we are a people who are *"zealous for good works"* (Titus 2:14)? What practical things can you be involved in around your community?

There are many ways of attempting to influence the authorities that we are subject to, other than voting and writing to politicians and civil servants. What are the merits for a Christian of the following methods:

- Protest marches, "sit-ins", etc?
- Silent protests, such as refusal to co-operate (such as Ghandi was famous for)?
- Lobbying government officials?
- Letters to the editor?
- Participating in radio phone-in shows?

Checkpoint – Exercizing your Rights

```
Would you participate in a public vote for or against
abortion, or gay rights, or going to war?
If your country declared war, would you enlist in the
armed forces? If it was compulsory would you register
as a 'conscientious objector' (the world sometimes
refers to them as "draft dodgers").
```

Shining Your Light

"You are the light of the world. A city that is set on a hill cannot be hidden. Nor do they light a lamp and hide it under a basket, but on a lampstand, and it gives light to all who are in the house. Let your light so shine before men, that they may see your good works arid glorify your Father in heaven" (Matthew 5:14-16).

In the first module we saw the significance in your own disciple life of the cross of Christ - that it is the dividing point between going your own way and going God's way. The cross is a crossroads. That requires you to think about taking that message to others. It is "the message of the cross": Paul said: *"For Christ did not send me to baptize, hut to preach the gospel, not with wisdom of words, lest the cross of Christ should be made of no effect. For the message of the cross is foolishness to those who are perishing, but to us who are being saved it is the power of God"* (1 Corinthians 1:17,18).

It is important when you proclaim (preach) the gospel (whether in public or in private), that you include in your preaching the full gospel of Jesus Christ (but not necessarily all at one time). You have been called to make disciples; their eternal salvation is a vital first step in this; but your job is not finished when they believe on Christ as their Saviour. Paul said: *"I have not shunned to declare to you the whole counsel of God"* (Acts 20:27).

Prayer is a vital part of your mission - that a door of opportunity will be opened for you that day: *"praying also for us, that God would open to us a door for the word, to speak the mystery of Christ, for which I am also in chains, that I may make it manifest, as I ought to speak"* (Colossians 4:3,4). It will reinforce your conviction and zeal for the task. It will remind you that you cannot catch 'fish" in your own strength. You can pray that those who are seeking God, whose hearts the Holy Spirit is already working in, will come to your attention, that you will be alert to see them and not too preoccupied with your own affairs, and that you will then be given the words to say.

Checkpoint - Light Check

Are you a "bushel believer", a "covered-up Christian", a "little-seen light"? Or are you a candle shining brightly in this dark world? We don't all have the gift of evangelism, but we can all be witnesses to what has happened to us.

A Need for Growth

"Enlarge the place of your tents and let them stretch out the curtains of your dwellings; do not spare; Lengthen your cords, and strengthen your stakes" (Isaiah 54:2).

We need to concern ourselves with growth in our church. Growth should occur in two directions - growth downward and growth outward. They go together. Growing deeper is growing stronger spiritually. Growing outward is growing larger. As the verse in Isaiah shows, the cords of a tent can only be lengthened to enlarge it to allow more people inside, if at the same time the stakes are being strengthened to hold the tent in place. As you and your church grow deeper in your experience with the Lord and obedience to Him, it should also be expressed in a focus on the need for enlargement. Impediments to growth need to be identified and dealt with. A focus on enlargement has two dimensions to it: (a) a ministry to other believers; and (b) a ministry to unbelievers.

A Ministry to Other Believers

"For the kingdom heaven is like a landowner who went out early in the morning to hire labourers for his vineyard" (Matthew 20:1). When the Bible talks about a vineyard, it is often a metaphor for the people of God in the house of God. We in the vineyard are to go out to recruit more workers for the vineyard.

We in churches of God benefit in many ways by other members of the body of Christ ministering to us - such as by their books and their hymns. But we have an obligation to minister to them - we have been given the truth of God's house which is very precious to God, Where else are other believers going to hear it if not from us? How many of us would have learned it if someone else had not taught it to us?

It is unlikely that a believer that you know will discover totally for themselves the truth of how God wants disciples to be gathered together in service for Him. And yet, as we saw it is a central part of God's purpose for them. Just as there are simplified approach to presenting the way of salvation to someone who is unsaved, so there is a simplified way to present the truth of God's house. It consists of 5 points:

1. **God wants believers to be united in service for Him.** While God makes us all different and gives us a diversity of gifts, there is not a diversity of truth. There is only one version of the truth of God, as contained in scripture, and the responsibility of each of us is to learn it and do it. In this respect it is no different than the way of salvation. (Ephesians 4:13; 1 Timothy 2:4)

2. **This unity can't be based just on salvation, on our personal preferences or cultural differences.** The Lord instructed His apostles before He left them to: *"Go therefore and make disciples of all the nations, baptizing them in the name of the Father and of the Son and of the Holy Spirit, teaching them to observe all things that I have commanded you"* (Matthew 28:19,20). Notice the emphasis on the "all things." ("Observe" means to "do.")

3. **The pattern for disciples gathering together is the churches of God that existed in the New Testament - a united "fellowship" of churches, governed by a united**

elderhood (1 Corinthians 1.9; 1 Peter 5.1,2; Acts 15:1,2; 16.4,5; Acts 20:28) This pattern was lost after the first century, but it has been regained in the last century and a bit.

4. **Disciples in these churches of God form the house of God, which is where God can be acceptably worshiped and served through Christ as high priest.** There can only be one house of God, by definition. The criterion is that it be '*the pillar and ground of the truth*" (1 Timothy 3:15). (See also Hebrews 36; 10:19-22; Ephesians 2:19-22).

5. **The only entrance requirements are salvation, baptism and addition.** However, a believer's place in it is conditional on their obedience (Acts 2:41,42; 1 Corinthians 5:13; Hebrews 3:6) This shows that it cannot be identical to the church the body of Christ, from which we cannot lose our place.

In attempting to present this truth to another believer, care needs to be taken to present it in a positive way, with support from Scripture, and to not give the impression of being critical of them. A Christian who does not know about the house of God is not being disobedient. Here are some other suggestions:

1. Don't be defensive because the Churches of God are small and this truth is not widely known. This is God's marvelous truth. In His sovereign grace He has shown it to you, and you want others to share in it as well. Try to let it show how precious it is to you.

2. Do not be critical of their present church affiliation. We are not entitled or equipped to do that. And it tends to offend people and interfere with what you are trying to

accomplish.

3. Try to avoid being drawn into a debate about practical reasons for choosing one church or another. Christians are often instructed to choose a good church, and so it is not surprising that they feel they have a free choice in the matter because all that matters is being saved and living a good individual Christian life. Try instead to always bring the conversation back to what the Scripture teaches.

4. Don't give the impression that we in the churches of God have reached perfection. If people come to see, they will be quickly disappointed.

5. Don't assume, or convey the impression, that they are being disobedient because they are not in the house of God. They may be more obedient relative to what they've been taught than we are.

6. Remember that you are just the messenger. You are not responsible for their reaction, nor are you a failure if you do not convince them. It is the Holy Spirit's work to convict them.

7. Don't feel that you have to have all the answers. Follow the 5-point outline, supporting each with a Scripture or two. You can always get help if necessary. It won't undermine what you are doing.

How do you respond when you are trying to show another believer about God's way of unity in churches of God and the response is: "That's the name of my church also" or "Isn't every church a church of God?" or "We do pretty well the same things you do" or "We think diversity of Christian denominations and traditions is a good thing that recognizes peoples' diversity and the freedom we have in Christ'?

Checkpoint – Your Experiences?

    Have you ever attempted to convince another believer
    about the churches of God? What happened?
    Do you feel able to do so? Do you think the 5-point
    outline will help?
    Is there a particular Christian friend that you have
    till you would like to share the truth of God's house
    with in this way?

A Ministry to Unbelievers

John chapters 3 and 4 give us two different examples of the Lord preaching to individuals. They are helpful models for us to use in different situations. In chapter 3 Nicodemus is a Jewish leader, very knowledgeable about the Old Testament, who came to Jesus to enquire of Him. In chapter 4, the woman at the well is not a Jew, and is a despised member of society with whom the Lord took the initiative in the conversation. It is useful to see the parallels to this in Paul's preaching. When he was speaking to knowledgeable Jews, he went into their synagogues and referred to the Old Testament, which they believed. With the pagan Greeks in Athens, on the other hand, lie started with their own religious traditions and linked them with what he wanted to tell them. In both cases He started with what people already knew and believed, and "bridged" to the gospel.

Are you an evangelist? Do you have the gift of evangelism? Then that is your calling and you have a particular mission to reach out to others with the truth of God. However, if you are not a gifted evangelist, you are still called to be a "witness" - to tell what you have experienced. Are you able to explain to a friend, in terms they can relate to, why you are saved arid why it is important to you to be a disciple of the Lord Jesus?

The gospel of salvation can also be presented in 5 simple steps, as follows:

1. We are all sinners and this is a barrier to us having a relationship with God, who is totally righteous (Romans 3:23; Ephesians 4:18).
2. The inevitable consequences of this sin is punishment and total separation from God (Matthew 23:33; John 3:36).
3. Jesus Christ is God's own Son, and the reason He came to this earth was to die in our place to bear God's punishment for our sin (1 Corinthians 15:3; 1 Peter 3:18).
4. If we accept this by faith, and acknowledge that He is our Saviour and Lord, God will then forgive all our sin and give us His gift of eternal life. It is futile to attempt to achieve favour with God by our own efforts. Rather than trying to be as good as we can be, we have to realize how bad we are by nature, and accept His remedy. It's the only way (John 3:16; Ephesians 2:8,9; Acts 4:12; Romans 10:9).
5. After receiving this salvation, we can never lose it, but God intends us to spend our lives from then on in obedience to Him. We need to learn from the Bible what this involves, usually with the help of a more mature Christian (John 10:28; 2 Corinthians 5:15; Matthew 28:18-20).

Checkpoint – How is Your Light Shining?

```
- What approach do you use in leading others to know
Christ? How effective is it?
- How can you use people's everyday needs and
problems, which is often what they want to talk
about, to lead to a witnessing opportunity?
- What are some of those needs? Are you able to show
from the Bible the relevance of the Lord to those
needs?
- How do people come into contact with you in a way
that gives you an opportunity to witness to them?
- What would you say to someone who said to you, "How
can I have the same faith that you have" or I don't
have a faith, although I go to church"? How would you
lead them to the point of salvation?
```

One approach is to have a personal story to tell from your own life that, at some point, refers to God and perhaps to answered prayer, and gives Him the credit. If you do it in a natural way, it may provoke a response that you can then use to lead them further. In conversation, if you ask people about themselves, and show a genuine interest in them they are usually willing to reciprocate by letting you tell them something about yourself, which can create an opening for what you want to say.

"whoever confesses Me before men, him I will also confess before My Father who is in heaven, but whoever denies Me before men, him I will also deny before My Father who is in heaven" (Matthew 10:32-33).

The older people are, often the harder it is for them to "unlearn" things that are contrary to God's way. They may have been brought up in a different religion, or strongly influenced by a particular philosophy of life. It may be hard for them to grasp what seems obvious to you. It requires a lot of patience and perseverance on your part But it is worth it.

Going Deeper – Making a Difference

The deeper you go in your personal spiritual life, the more it will be apparent to others. People will notice. It might bring persecution, or resentment, or admiration. But it will have an effect on people one way or another. That is our mission. You can make a difference in this world by being a preservative salt, and by being a truth-giving light. We are Christ's ambassadors until He comes back.

"... God was in Christ reconciling the world to Himself, not imputing their trespasses to them, and has committed to us the word of reconciliation. Now therefore, we are ambassadors for Christ, as though God were pleading through us" (2 Corinthians 5:19,20).

About Hayes Press

Hayes Press (www.hayespress.org) is a registered charity in the United Kingdom, whose primary mission is to disseminate the Word of God, mainly through literature. It is one of the largest distributors of gospel tracts and leaflets in the United Kingdom, with over 100 titles and many thousands dispatched annually. In addition to paperbacks and eBooks, Hayes Press also publishes Golden Bells, a popular daily Bible reading calendar

If you would like to contact Hayes Press, there are a number of ways you can do so:

- By mail: c/o The Barn, Flaxlands, Royal Wootton Bassett, Wiltshire, UK SN4 8DY
- By phone: 01793 850598
- By eMail: info@hayespress.org
- via Facebook: www.facebook.com/hayespress.org

More Books from Hayes Press

Hayes Press has published hundreds of books and here's just a sample of them by topic:

Module-based Courses with Study Questions

- The Believer's Position and the Disciple's Practice - Ephesians
- Transformed by the Gospel – Romans
- Serving Acceptably – Hebrews
- Growing Disciples – A Bible Study Course for Followers of Jesus
- The Call of Christ – Living Life to the Full
- Different Discipleship – The Sermon on the Mount

Apologetics

- If Atheism is True... The Futile Faith and Hopeless Hypotheses of Dawkins & Co.
- Incredible Unbelief ... When Believing Nothing Means Believing Anything
- Overcoming Objections to Christian Faith

Church Truth

- Where is God's House Today?
- Uncovering the Pattern
- The Breaking of the Bread: Its History, Its Observance, Its Meaning
- Living in God's House - His Design in Action
- Walking With God: Principles of Separation in Christian Life and Service

Jesus Christ

- More Than a Saviour: Exploring the Person and Work of Jesus
- Heavenly Meanings - The Parables of Jesus
- Sparkling Facets - The Names and Titles of Jesus
- Jesus - What Does the Bible Really Say?

Moral & Ethical Issues

- Alive to God
- Exploring Issues of Life

Character Studies

- Lessons from Elijah and Elisha
- Fisherman to Follower - The Life and Teachings of Simon Peter
- The Life of King David - From Shepherd Boy to Sovereign
- Lessons from Ezra and Nehemiah

Bible Book Studies

- 1 Corinthians - Nothing But Christ Crucified
- Ezekiel Explained - Getting to Know God
- Possessing the Land - Spiritual Lessons from Joshua
- Exploring the Psalms (4 volumes)
- Unlocking Hebrews

Bible Prophecy

- Daniel Decoded - Deciphering Bible Prophecy
- The Future in Bible Prophecy
- The Finger of Prophecy
- A Study in Prophetic Principles

Devotional

- The View from Goak Hill - A Christian's Perspective on Life and Living
- Light from Darke (3 volumes)
- A Little Book About Being Christlike
- Knowing God - Reflections on Psalm 23
- Grace for Today - A Daily Devotional

General Theology

- The Hidden Christ - Types and Shadows (4 volumes)
- Blood Most Precious - A Bible Study
- The Holy Spirit and the Believer
- Once Saved, Always Saved - The Reality of Eternal Security
- Sacrifices and Offerings Under the Old Covenant